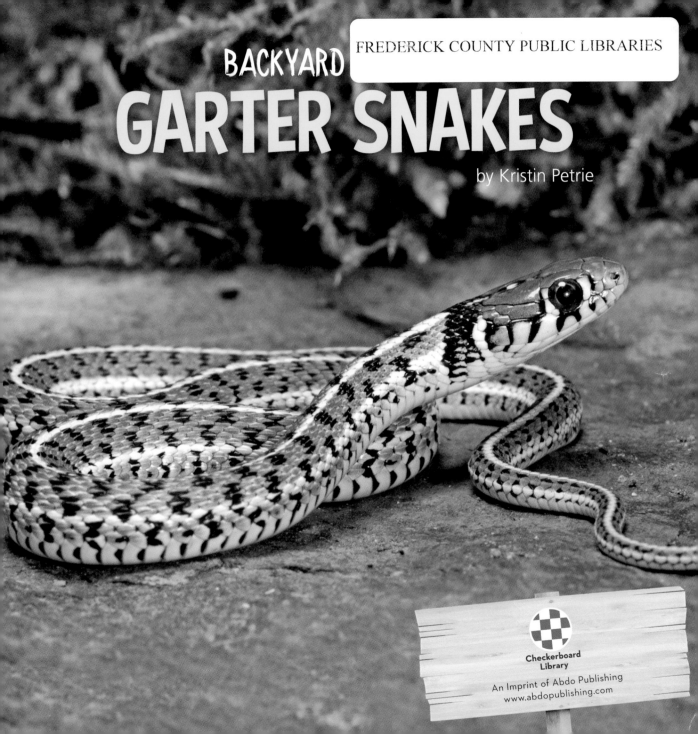

BACKYARD
GARTER SNAKES

by Kristin Petrie

Checkerboard Library

An Imprint of Abdo Publishing
www.abdopublishing.com

www.abdopublishing.com

Published by Abdo Publishing, a division of ABDO, PO Box 398166, Minneapolis, Minnesota 55439.
Copyright © 2015 by Abdo Consulting Group, Inc. International copyrights reserved in all countries. No part of this
book may be reproduced in any form without written permission from the publisher. Checkerboard Library™ is a
trademark and logo of Abdo Publishing.

Printed in the United States of America, North Mankato, Minnesota.
102014
012015

THIS BOOK CONTAINS
RECYCLED MATERIALS

Cover Photos: iStockphoto, Science Source
Interior Photos: Alamy pp. 1, 14, 24, 29; Glow Images pp. 6, 12, 17, 19; iStockphoto pp. 5, 9, 15, 25; JIM
      BRANDENBURG/MINDEN PICTURES/National Geographic Creative p. 13; NORBERT ROSING/National
      Geographic Creative pp. 20–21; Science Source pp. 10, 11, 22, 26–27

Series Coordinator: Megan M. Gunderson
Editor: Rochelle Baltzer
Art Direction: Neil Klinepier

Library of Congress Cataloging-in-Publication Data

Petrie, Kristin, 1970- author.
  Garter snakes / Kristin Petrie.
      pages cm. -- (Backyard animals)
  Audience: Ages 8-12.
  Includes index.
  ISBN 978-1-62403-660-6
1. Garter snakes--Juvenile literature. I. Title.
  QL666.O636P48 2015
  597.96'2--dc23
                        2014024642

TABLE OF CONTENTS

GARTER SNAKES

What slithering creature is feared by countless humans? This reptile lacks arms and legs. Yet it moves quickly, and it causes people to run even faster. This creature is the snake!

One type of snake is the garter snake. These snakes are from the scientific family Colubridae. They make up the genus *Thamnophis*, which includes more than 30 different species.

These include the plains garter snake, the western terrestrial garter snake, the blackneck garter snake, and the Butler's garter snake. There are also longnose, shorthead, and giant garter snakes.

The common garter snake is the species *sirtalis*. There are several subspecies within this group. These include Texas, Chicago, red-sided, and blue-stripe garter snakes.

Garter snakes are cold-blooded, **vertebrate** reptiles. They live in wooded areas, wetlands, gardens, and of course, backyards! Keep reading to learn more about the slithering, widespread garter snake.

SCIENTIFIC CLASSIFICATION

Kingdom: Animalia
Phylum: Chordata
Class: Reptilia
Order: Squamata
Family: Colubridae
Genus: *Thamnophis*

More than half of all snake species belong to the family Colubridae.

WHAT'S IN A NAME?
Garter snakes belong to the genus *Thamnophis*. This word is from Greek. *Thamn* means "shrub" or "bush" and *ophis* means "snake."

WHERE THEY LIVE

The garter snake is found in much of the Western **Hemisphere**. These snakes live from coast to coast in the United States. They are found north into Canada. They live as far south as Central America.

Within this large geographic area there are many different types of **habitats**. Wetlands, marshes, forests, and other damp places are preferred. So, garter snakes are often confused with water snakes. City parks, backyards, and gardens also provide good habitats. For this reason, garter snakes are sometimes called "garden snakes."

Ideal habitats have places for hiding and denning. Garter snakes generally find small spaces in rock piles, under boards, in fallen trees, or underground for their dens. Snakes also use dens for sleeping and winter **hibernation**.

The red-sided garter snake is found in northern Canada. It lives farther north than any other reptile in the Western Hemisphere.

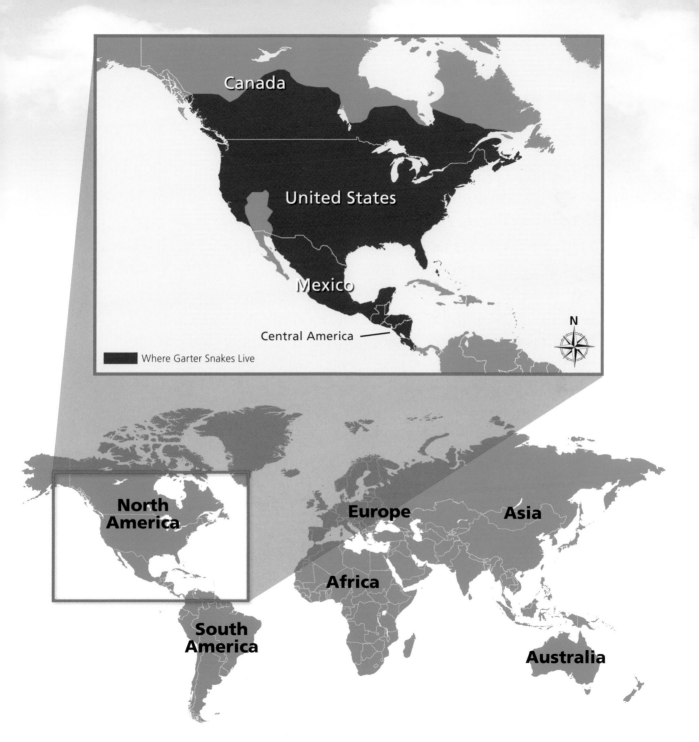

Canada

United States

Mexico

Central America

N

Where Garter Snakes Live

North America

South America

Europe

Asia

Africa

Australia

HEAD TO TAIL

Garter snakes are long and narrow. Males are shorter and thinner than females. But, they may have longer tails. Garter snakes are generally less than 39 inches (100 cm) long. The average common garter snake measures 18 to 54 inches (46 to 137 cm) long. It weighs just over 5 ounces (140 g).

Garter snake species offer a wide variety of colors and patterns. Their bodies range from gray to brown to black to olive or dark green with a lighter belly.

Usually, three stripes run the length of the garter snake's body. There is one in the middle of the back and one on each side. However, a garter snake may have just one stripe or no stripes. Stripes may be yellow, red, blue, or orange.

Some garter snake species have a checkered appearance. Others look spotted. Some are a solid color. Many have two yellow or white spots on top of the head. These patterns come from the colors of the garter snake's overlapping scales.

SOCKS & SNAKES
Garter snakes get their name from the garter, which is a strap used to hold up a sock.

THE GARTER SNAKE

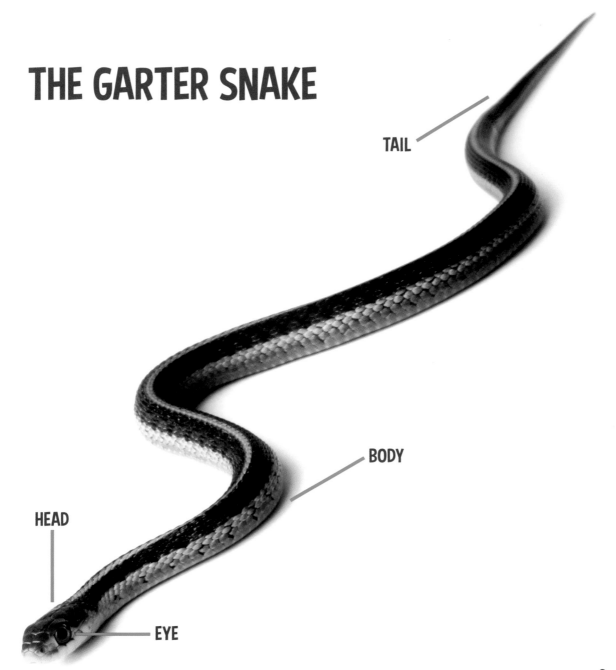

TAIL

BODY

HEAD

EYE

A snake's scales look dull right before it sheds. Afterward, the snake returns to its shinier look.

The garter snake's body is **dense** and narrow. This shape affects how a snake's internal **organs** are arranged. In a person, organs such as the kidneys are each on one side of the body. In a snake, they are one in front of the other!

Some garter snake species have larger heads than others. For example, the common garter snake's head is wider than its neck. The Butler's garter snake's head is about the same size as its neck.

A garter snake may hide more as it gets ready to molt. This helps protect it when its vision is cloudy as its scales loosen.

The garter snake has a forked tongue. The tongue is usually red with two black tips. The garter snake's eyes are set on either side of the head. This gives the snake a wide field of view. When the snake is ready to **molt**, the scales over its eyes get cloudy.

Snakes molt, or shed, as they grow. Young garter snakes molt often because they grow rapidly. Older garter snakes continue shedding at a slower pace. A garter snake grows throughout its entire lifetime.

SNAKESKIN
A healthy snake sheds its skin in one big piece.

SEEKING A MEAL

Snakes are well known for eating creatures much bigger than themselves. Many pictures show a python or an anaconda with half of a mouse, frog, or bird sticking out of its mouth. Other pictures show snakes with the outline of entire animals within their bodies.

Snakes are carnivores, and they do eat large animals such as these. However, a snake's diet depends on what is available in its **habitat**. Favorite meals also differ by species.

Most snakes feed on smaller prey. Since garter snakes often live near water, their diet may include minnows and other small fish.

Garter snakes and much of their prey live in and around water.

This common garter snake has clearly eaten a large meal!

They also eat frogs, toads, and tadpoles. Garter snakes seek out earthworms, slugs, snails, leeches, and various insects. They eat salamanders, small mammals, birds, other snakes, and even **carrion**.

A New Mexico garter snake
swallowing its catch

Not all snakes rely on seeing. But most garter snakes have a decent sense of sight.

Garter snakes hunt their prey using their keen senses. They have an excellent sense of smell. Sticking their tongues in the air, these snakes detect the scent of another animal. They can also sense vibrations. These reveal a prey animal's movement, size, and location.

To catch prey, the garter snake may use methods such as watching, peering, craning, stalking, chasing, or ambushing. Snakes ambush their targets with speed and **accuracy**. Prey is held in place with the garter snake's teeth. Small prey can be controlled by the garter snake's slightly toxic bite.

Like other snakes, the garter snake eats its prey whole. A flexible jaw and many movable bones in the skull allow it to eat large objects. Snakes may seek out a warm place in the sun when **digesting** a meal.

ALL YOU CAN EAT

Snakes eat such large meals that they use a lot of energy to digest their food. Because of this, their internal organs may shrink! These must return to normal size when the snake gets hungry again.

HOW THEY ACT

The time of day a garter snake is most active depends on its **habitat**. Garter snakes are usually **diurnal**. This means they are most active during daylight hours. In very hot weather, they may be **nocturnal**. On warm winter days, they may lie on rocks and bask in the sun.

Mornings are often spent warming in the sun. This helps the cold-blooded animal keep its body temperature around 82 to 90 degrees Fahrenheit (28° to 32°C) for the day. Other daytime hours are spent looking for food.

In late fall, some garter snakes leave their summer breeding grounds for winter dens. These areas can be far from one another, requiring **migration**. Like summer dens, winter dens are located under rock piles, in tree stumps, or in the burrows of other animals. The snakes use them for **hibernation**.

During hibernation, the garter snake's body temperature and heart rate drop. This conserves energy, which allows for long periods of rest. Garter snakes hibernate in large piles. They lie together and form tight coils to maintain body heat.

Garter snakes peeking out of their den

MAKE ROOM
Butler's and eastern garter snakes may share their hibernation site.

SENSES & COMMUNICATION

Garter snakes use their senses to communicate and pick up information. For example, the garter snake can sense movement and vibration. It has no outer ears. But, its skull bones pick up sound waves that go to the inner ears. This helps the garter snake sense what is around, approaching, or pursuing it.

Garter snakes also use chemical signals called pheromones (FEHR-uh-mohnz) in communication. Pheromones are given off from their skin. Another snake can absorb the pheromone trail through its tongue.

The snake sticks out its tongue, picks up the odor, and brings its tongue back into its mouth. There, the tongue touches two hollow areas on the roof of the mouth. This allows the special Jacobson's **organ** to decode the odors and give the snake information.

Pheromones carry many messages. For example, they allow baby snakes to find other snakes and food. Also, males and females give off and pick up pheromones that help attract mates.

A garter snake's tongue picks up odors from the air and from things it actually touches.

BABY SNAKES

Garter snakes usually breed one time per year in the spring. However, species such as the western terrestrial garter snake are known to mate in the fall. In spring, a mating ritual begins immediately after the **hibernating** snakes come out of their den.

For example, male common garter snakes leave the den first. Then, they wait for the females. Their bodies are releasing pheromones at this point. These attract the female snakes.

When all females have come out, the males surround them. Each female then selects a male for mating. After mating, female common garter snakes move back to their summer homes. Males remain near the den to breed with other females.

Garter snakes are known to gather in large groups when ready to mate.

A mother garter snake leaves her babies to survive on their own.

Female garters are ovoviviparous (oh-voh-veye-VIH-puh-ruhs). This means they carry and give birth to live snakes. They do not lay eggs. Instead, baby garter snakes grow inside their mother until birth.

Female garter snakes are **pregnant** until summer. They give birth to large **litters**. Litter size depends on nutrition, where the mother lives, and her size. Some species give birth to up to 80 little snakes! The average is 18 baby snakes. Common garter snakes usually have 10 to 40 babies at once.

Baby garter snakes are fully independent at birth. The father is not involved in their birth. And, the mother does not care for them or protect them after birth.

For these reasons, a lot of baby garter snakes do not survive. Many common garter snakes die within their first year of life. Females living beyond their first year are ready to reproduce when they are 2 years old. Males can reproduce slightly earlier, at 1.5 years of age. On average, garter snakes in nature live about 2 years. In captivity, they have lived more than 10 years.

DID YOU KNOW?
Most snake species lay eggs.

ENEMIES & DEFENSES

Why do wild garter snakes have such short lives? They have a large number of natural predators. Predators differ by region and **habitat**. For example, garter snakes living in very wet areas such as swamps and marshes have water-loving predators. These include bullfrogs, snapping turtles, and large fish. Other snakes also prey on garter snakes. Coral, milk, and king snakes are a threat.

The great blue heron is one enemy of the garter snake.

A snake's first line of defense is to stay hidden.

Predators from above include crows, hawks, bald eagles, and great blue herons. On the ground, foxes, squirrels, raccoons, and shrews pursue garter snakes. Coyotes, minks, opossums, skunks, weasels, and **domestic** cats are also a threat.

The garter snake's best defense is to remain invisible! The snake's scales act as camouflage. This helps it blend into surroundings and avoid being spotted. The snake's stripes also make it hard for predators to keep it in sight, especially in grass.

When being chased, the garter snake may head for water. This leaves many predators frustrated on land. When escape is not possible, the garter snake will hide its head and shake its tail. Or these small, fearless creatures will coil their bodies for a larger, meaner look. The garter will also flatten its body on the ground.

When all else fails, the garter snake will strike out and bite its pursuer. This may startle or scare off the predator. That gives the garter snake another chance to escape.

Garter snakes secrete a mild **venom**. The venom helps them slow down and kill their small prey. It is not usually dangerous to humans unless the person is allergic to it.

This venom does not go in with a single bite. Rather, the garter snake gets the venom into its prey or predator by chewing.

If a garter snake is seized, it flings its body around in an attempt to escape. No luck? The garter snake also releases a nasty-smelling secretion. And, it may even pee or poop on its attacker!

A garter snake bite is generally just mildly irritating to humans. But, it should still be checked out by a doctor!

WHO'S THAT?

In many areas, the garter snake is the type of snake people are most likely to see.

SNAKES AT RISK?

Unfortunately, the garter snake also faces several human-made challenges. Deforestation, construction, and other land clearing are its greatest threats. These activities destroy the snake's **habitat**. They decrease its food supply as well.

Direct contact with **pesticides** can be harmful. In addition, pesticides that end up in water can cause problems. Much of the garter snake's diet consists of creatures that may be harmed by these chemicals.

Humans also collect wild or captive-bred garter snakes to keep as pets. And, snakes are killed by people who consider them pests or dangerous. They are at risk from cars, too.

Despite their challenges, most garter snake species are thriving. The **IUCN** considers a few species vulnerable or **endangered**. The giant garter snake is one species at risk.

Garter snakes play an important role in nature. They control the population of many insects and other pests. This is a welcome service for gardeners and crop growers. Lastly, the garter snake plays an important role in the food chain. So, keep an eye out for these important reptiles in your neighborhood!

The San Francisco garter snake is endangered.

THEY'RE EVERYWHERE!
Most states in the United States are home to at least one species of garter snake.

GLOSSARY

accuracy - the state of being free from errors.

carrion - dead, rotting animal flesh.

dense - thick or compact.

digest - to break down food into simpler substances the body can absorb. Digestion is the process of digesting.

diurnal (deye-UHR-nuhl) - active during the day.

domestic - tame, especially relating to animals.

endangered - in danger of becoming extinct.

habitat - the place where a living thing is naturally found.

hemisphere - one half of Earth.

hibernate - to spend a period of time, such as the winter, in deep sleep.

IUCN - the International Union for Conservation of Nature. The IUCN is a global environmental organization focused on conservation.

litter - all of the babies born to a mother snake at one time.

migration - moving from one place to another, often to find food.

molt - to shed skin, hair, or feathers and replace with new growth.

nocturnal - active at night.

organ - a part of an animal or a plant composed of several kinds of tissues. An organ performs a specific function. Organs of an animal include the heart, the brain, and the eyes.

pesticide (PEHS-tuh-side) - a substance used to destroy pests.

pregnant - having one or more babies growing within the body.

venom - a poison produced by some animals and insects. It usually enters a victim through a bite or a sting.

vertebrate (VUHR-tuh-bruht) - having a backbone.

WEBSITES

To learn more about Backyard Animals,
visit **booklinks.abdopublishing.com**. These links are routinely monitored and updated to provide the most current information available.

INDEX